This little birthday
book belongs to

Raelynn   _4/93_

Happy
Birthday!!
To my best
Buddy
Love You
Mug

SOMETHING TELLS ME IT'S YOUR BIRTHDAY...

Another Birthday?

by
Mary Engelbreit

Andrews and McMeel
A Universal Press Syndicate Company
Kansas City

10 9 8 7 6 5 4 3 2

ISBN: 0-8362-4603-9

Library of Congress Catalog Card Number: 91-78255

Another Birthday?

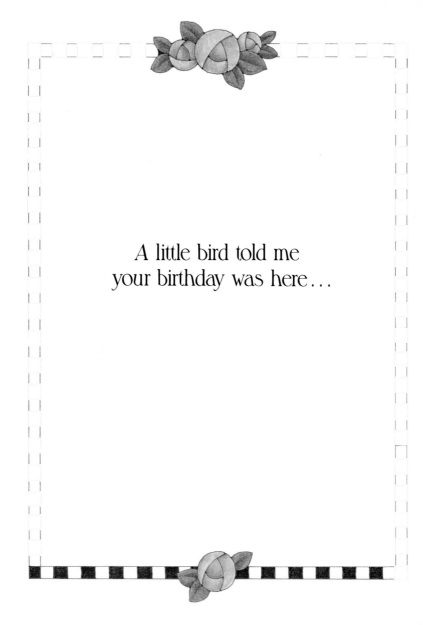

A little bird told me
your birthday was here...

PATTY·CAKE, PATTY·CAKE, BAKER'S MAN
BAKE ME A CAKE AS FAST AS YOU CAN
PIT IT & PAT IT · MARK IT WITH A ·· B ···
PUT IT IN THE OVEN FOR MICHAEL & ME

That really great,
celebrate
day of the year—

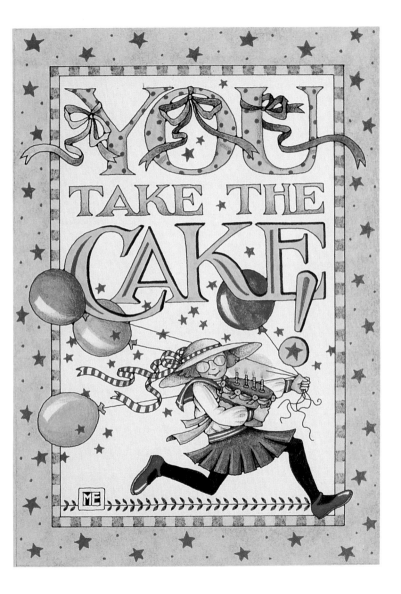

A day meant for others
to give unto you...

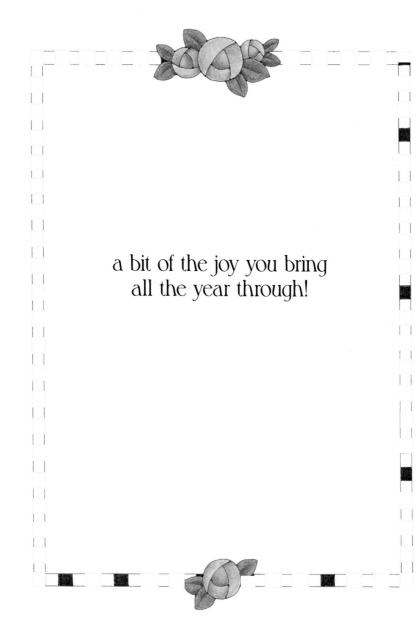

a bit of the joy you bring
all the year through!

HOW DO YOUR CANDLES GLOW?

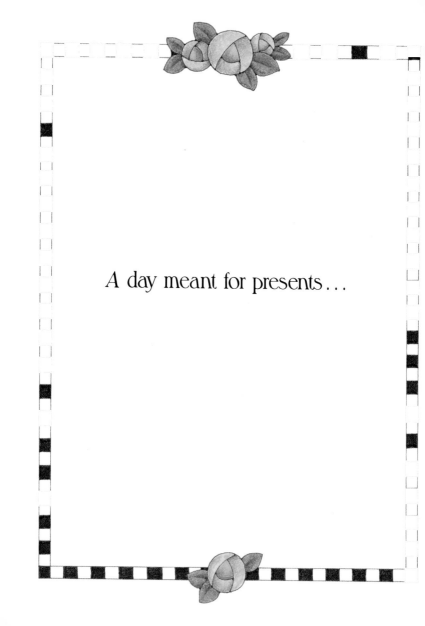

A day meant for presents…

for bright candleglow . . .

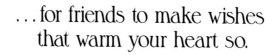

...for friends to make wishes
that warm your heart so.

MAKE · A · WISH

A day meant for dreaming
of what lies ahead…

BIRTHDAY WISHES

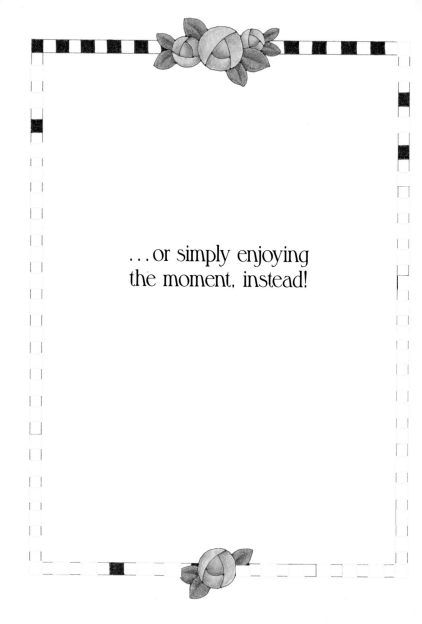

...or simply enjoying
the moment, instead!

KING OF THE

ME

IRTHDAYS

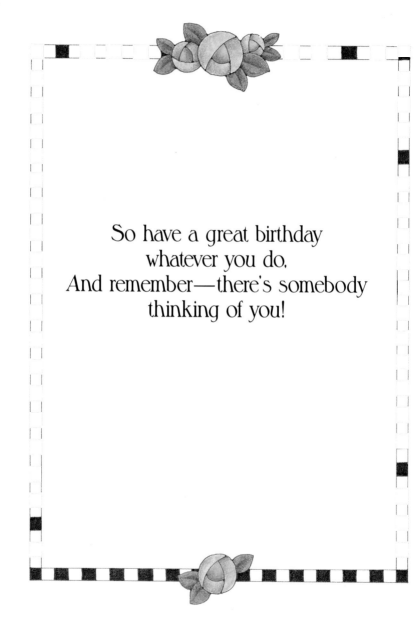

So have a great birthday
whatever you do,
And remember—there's somebody
thinking of you!